THE *Maryland* COLONY

Our Thirteen Colonies

SPIRIT
of America®

THE *Maryland* COLONY

By Jean Kinney Williams

Content Adviser: Eric Gilg, Department of History, University of
Massachusetts, Amherst, Massachusetts

The Child's World®
Chanhassen, Minnesota

Central Islip Public Library
33 Hawthorne Avenue
Central Islip, NY 11722

2104905

6

THE *Maryland* COLONY

Published in the United States of America by The Child's World®
PO Box 326 • Chanhassen, MN 55317-0326 • 800-599-READ • www.childsworld.com

Acknowledgments
The Child's World®: Mary Berendes, Publishing Director

Editorial Directions, Inc.: E. Russell Primm, Editorial Director; Melissa McDaniel, Line Editor; Elizabeth K. Martin, Assistant Editor; Olivia Nellums, Editorial Assistant; Susan Hindman, Copy Editor; Joanne Mattern, Proofreader; Kevin Cunningham, Peter Garnham, Ruthanne Swiatkowski, Fact Checkers; Tim Griffin/IndexServ, Indexer; Cian Loughlin O'Day, Photo Researcher; Linda S. Koutris, Photo Selector

Photo
Cover: Bettmann/Corbis; Bettmann/Corbis: 15, 17, 20, 22, 24, 25, 34; Bridgeman Art Library: 8 (The Stapleton Collection), 18 (Philip Mould, Historical Pictures Ltd.), 29 (Yale Center for British Art/Paul Mellon Collections); Corbis: 11, 28; Getty Images/Hulton Archive: 12, 19, 32, 33; The Mariner's Museum/Corbis: 6, 9; Maryland State Archive: 16, 26, 29, 30; North Wind Picture Archives: 10, 13, 14, 23, 35. Stock Montage: 27.

Registration
The Child's World®, Spirit of America®, and their associated logos are the sole property and registered trademarks of The Child's World®.

Copyright ©2004 by The Child's World®. All rights reserved. No part of this book may be reproduced or utilized in any form or by any means without written permission from the publisher.

Library of Congress Cataloging-in-Publication Data
Williams, Jean Kinney.
  The Maryland Colony / by Jean Kinney Williams.
    p. cm. — (Our colonies)
"Spirit of America."
Summary: Relates the history of the Colony of Maryland from its founding by Cecil Calvert in 1634 to its statehood in 1788 and donation of land and money for the new nation's capital in 1791. Includes bibliographical references (p.) and index.
  ISBN 1-56766-615-9 (alk. paper)
  1. Maryland—History—Colonial period, ca. 1600–1775—Juvenile literature. 2. Maryland—History—1775–1865—Juvenile literature. [1. Maryland—History—Colonial period, ca. 1600–1775. 2. Maryland—History—1775–1865.] I. Title. II. Series.
  F184.W55 2003
  975.2'02—dc21   2003003770

Contents

Chapter ONE

Maryland's First People

Many early explorers and adventurers created paintings and drawings that today show Native Americans appeared to the Europeans of long ago.

THE FIRST PEOPLE ARRIVED IN THE AREA NOW called Maryland about 12,000 years ago. You might say they were Maryland's first "colonists." These native people were hunters, who moved around following wild animals. Maryland's Native Americans began forming villages about 1,000 years ago along Chesapeake Bay.

It was a good place to settle, since food was plentiful. There were woods for hunting, rich soil for growing corn, and lots of fish and seafood in the bay and rivers. Maryland's Native Americans

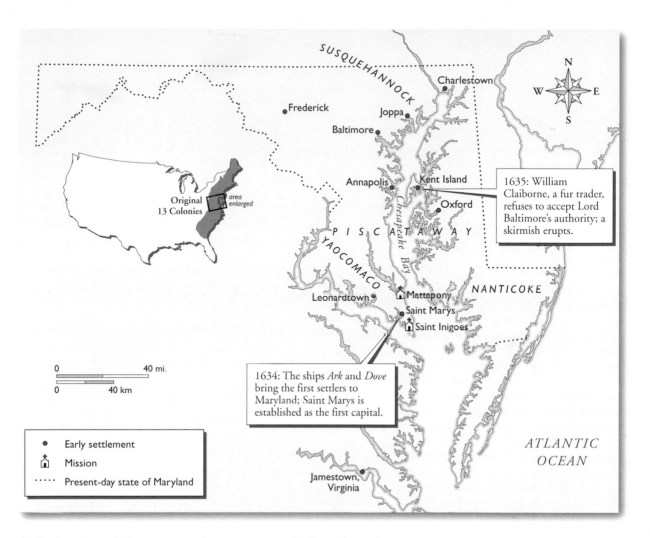

Maryland Colony at the time of the first European settlement

Map labels:

SUSQUEHANNOCK

Charlestown

Frederick

Joppa

Baltimore

Annapolis   Kent Island

1635: William Claiborne, a fur trader, refuses to accept Lord Baltimore's authority; a skirmish erupts.

Oxford

Chesapeake Bay

PISCATAWAY

YAOCOMACO

NANTICOKE

Leonardtown   Mattapony

Saint Marys

Saint Inigoes

1634: The ships *Ark* and *Dove* bring the first settlers to Maryland; Saint Marys is established as the first capital.

ATLANTIC OCEAN

Jamestown, Virginia

Original 13 Colonies   area enlarged

0   40 mi.
0   40 km

Legend:
- Early settlement
- Mission
- Present-day state of Maryland

left behind large garbage pits full of crab and oyster shells.

By the 1500s, the Nanticoke, Pocomoke, Wicomico, Piscataway, Patuxent, and other groups lived along the bay. These were all Algonquian peoples, who spoke similar languages and had similar customs. But moving down from the north were their enemies, a people called the Susquehannock. The Susquehannock waged war against the

Interesting Fact

▸ *Chesapeake* is a Native American word that means "great shellfish bay."

7

other Native Americans in order to take control of their lands.

Most native people in Maryland were friendly toward the first European settlers in the region. They lived peacefully with the Europeans, hoping that the settlers would help protect them from the Susquehannock. When the European newcomers formed an **assembly** to make laws, their Native American neighbors attended the meetings. They discussed complaints, such as white settlers using native land for hunting or building homes.

This detail from a larger drawing shows a warrior from the Susquehannock tribe. The Susquehannocks lived in a wide region of the east coast and waged war on the Algonquin tribes.

Despite this relative peace, however, the Native Americans suffered as a result of European settlement. They caught diseases such as measles and smallpox from the European settlers. These diseases were common in Europe, so Europeans' bodies could fight them. But the Native Americans had never been exposed to them before. The native population in Maryland was greatly reduced. Across North America, millions of Native Americans died.

As more and more Europeans arrived in Maryland, the colony's Native Americans moved west and north, some as far as Canada. By the 1740s, no native groups remained in Maryland.

Interesting Fact

▸ When Leonard Calvert arrived in Maryland in 1634, the Piscataway tribe included nearly 2,000 members. By 1675, only about 150 of them remained.

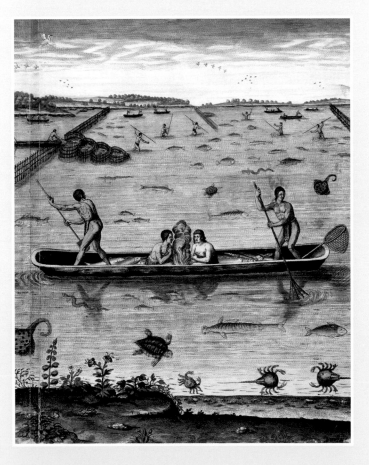

Native American Life

NATIVE AMERICANS IN MARYLAND lived in wigwams, round huts with walls made of tree bark. They used shells for money. They also formed axes from stone and made pottery from clay that they dug from the earth. The native people of Maryland wove beautiful mats and baskets.

The men were very skilled at building canoes and making nets to catch seafood. Women tended the crops such as corn, beans, and squash. They also gathered clams, oysters, berries, and nuts.

Chapter Two

The New Colony

The men who sailed to America on the Ark *and the* Dove *had high hopes of finding religious freedom away from England. They wanted to make Maryland a safe place for Roman Catholics.*

IN MARCH 1634, TWO ENGLISH SHIPS, THE *Ark* and the *Dove*, sailed into Chesapeake Bay. Aboard were 20 young **noblemen** and about 200 workers. They were going to help build a new colony.

The noblemen were Roman Catholic. They had left Protestant England to find religious freedom in North America. They had received large grants of land in Maryland. Workers, both men and women, who had paid their own travel expenses received smaller amounts of land. Other workers on

LEONARD CALVERT PLANTING THE FIRST COLONY IN MARYLAND.

the ships were **indentured servants.** They would receive land in exchange for a few years of their labor. Though the leaders of the colony were Catholic, most of the first settlers were Protestant.

The new colony belonged to a Catholic nobleman named Cecilius Calvert, whose title was Lord Baltimore. England's King Charles I had given Cecilius's father, George Calvert, a **charter** for a new colony called Maryland. George Calvert wanted to establish a place where Catholics could worship freely. When he died suddenly, 26-year-old Cecilius became Lord Baltimore and owner of Maryland. Cecilius's younger brother Leonard, who traveled with the first group of settlers, was Maryland's first governor. Lord Baltimore stayed in England to keep an eye on his political enemies.

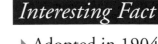

Interesting Fact

▶ Adopted in 1904, Maryland's flag is one of the oldest in the nation. Its design and bold colors come from symbols used by the family of Cecelius Calvert, the first Lord Baltimore.

After converting to Catholicism, George Calvert resigned from his government job in England. He hoped to create an American colony for Catholics, but it was his sons who ended up fulfilling that dream.

▶ The Chesapeake Bay
was formed 10,000 years
ago when melting gla-
ciers caused the Atlantic
Ocean to rise. When
the water flowed into
the Susquehanna River,
its banks overflowed,
and a bay was created.

Father Andrew White, a Catholic priest
traveling with the first settlers, called Chesapeake Bay "the most delightful water I ever
saw." The two ships sailed into the bay and
a short way up the Potomac River, where the
Yaocomaco people lived. They gave the Yaocomaco hoes, cloth, and axes in exchange for
their land. The Yaocomaco were glad to sell
their village and move away from their
enemies, the Susquehannock.

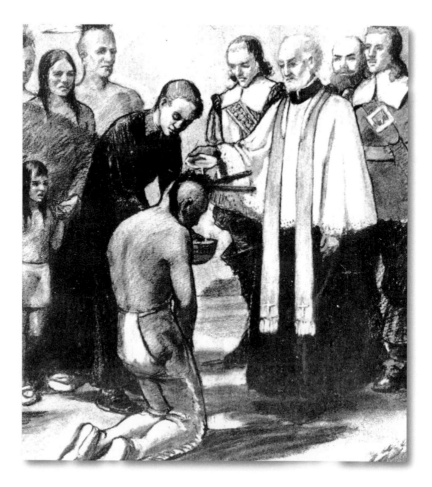

Father Andrew White, a
Catholic priest, was glad
to get away from Protestant
England. In the new world
of America he baptized some
of the Native Americans
into the Catholic faith.

The new settlement was named Saint Marys. The friendly Yaocomaco helped the people of Saint Marys plant corn. That fall, enough corn was harvested to send a large ship ment to settlers in Massachusetts in exchange for salted fish and other supplies. Maryland's settlers also did business with local Native Americans, buying or trading for fishing nets and canoes. Lord Baltimore bought enough woven mats from the Native Americans to carpet his home in England.

The early years of the Saint Marys settlement were marked by cooperation between Native Americans and colonists.

The colonists built cabins and planted wheat, corn, and tobacco. Maryland's charter said that the colonists would owe the king no taxes. Instead, the colonists who owned land paid rent to Lord Baltimore in wheat and tobacco.

Lord Baltimore told the settlers to live peacefully with other colonists and Native

Americans. It was another Englishman in Maryland, William Claiborne, who gave the settlers in Saint Marys trouble. A fur-trader living on nearby Kent Island, Claiborne did not accept Lord Baltimore's power over the colony. A small battle erupted between Claiborne and the new settlers in 1635, and at one point Claiborne tried to take control of the colony.

Maryland's landowners formed a General Assembly in 1635. They passed laws and sent them to Lord Baltimore for approval. He

William Claiborne tried to maintain the independence of his Kent Island trading post in Chesapeake Bay. But his conflicts with Lord Baltimore are a well-known part of history.

vetoed, or rejected, them, saying it was his job to write laws. After a few years, Baltimore allowed his brother Leonard, who was the governor, to approve the assembly's laws. One law they all agreed upon was the Act of Religious Toleration. Passed in 1649, it promised freedom of worship to all Christians in the colony. Religious freedom would one day be an important right for all Americans.

Maryland grew as people in England learned about the good farmland there and the chance to worship as they wished. Saint Marys remained the colony's main town.

Tobacco soon became an important crop. Sometimes it was even used as money. In time, tobacco growers replaced their log cabins with stately brick homes.

Claiborn, shown here, was a Protestant. His rebellion convinced Lord Baltimore that more control was needed over the colony.

WHEN GOVERNOR LEONARD CALVERT DIED IN 1647, A WOMAN NAMED MARGARET Brent was put in charge of his estate, or property and money. Brent had arrived in Maryland in 1638. She paid her own travel expenses, as well as those of several other people, so she received a large piece of land. Brent earned a reputation as a good property manager. Because of this reputation, she was put in charge of Calvert's estate. This was an unusual job for a woman in those days.

Margaret Brent claimed the right to vote in the General Assembly, but the new governor, Thomas Greene, refused to allow it. But she did help the colony through a crisis. Some soldiers from Virginia had helped Marylanders fight off a band of Susquehannock and Nanticoke. However, Governor Calvert died before he could pay the soldiers as he'd promised. They threatened to rebel if they didn't get paid, and the new governor didn't know what to do. Margaret Brent met with the soldiers to calm them down. Then she sold enough of Calvert's property and cattle to pay them. The assembly reported to Lord Baltimore that Margaret Brent had rescued the young colony.

Chapter THREE

Struggle and Growth

Charles Calvert, the third Lord Baltimore, became governor of the Maryland colony when his father, Cecilius, died.

CECILIUS CALVERT DIED IN 1675 AFTER owning Maryland for 41 years. His son Charles, who was Maryland's governor, became the new Lord Baltimore. The Calvert family remained the owners of Maryland for another 100 years.

Over time, religious conflicts in England seeped into Maryland. In 1692, the Church of England became Maryland's official religion, and the Act of Religious Toleration was put aside.

In 1694, Annapolis, named for England's Queen Anne, became the new capital of the colony. Like Saint Marys, Annapolis was a small town, but it was more centrally located than Saint Marys.

To the north was a new colony, Pennsylvania. As in Maryland, Pennsylvania protected religious freedom. Though tolerant toward many religions, people in Maryland and Pennsylvania argued with each other over the border between the two colonies. In 1767, the dispute was finally settled when the Mason-Dixon Line was drawn. The Mason-Dixon Line later became the unofficial line between the northern and southern states.

In the 1600s and 1700s, life in Maryland revolved around the tobacco **plantations.**

Without its highly successful tobacco industry, the Maryland colony would never have grown so rapidly or had the money it needed to support itself. Unfortunately, slave labor was required to make the plantations so successful.

19

There was no end to the work colonial woman had to take care of every day. Working at the hearth was dangerous as sparks from the fire often set a woman's dress on fire.

Hardworking indentured servants built homes alongside wealthy landowners. Clusters of smaller homes grew around the large houses that dotted the countryside.

Most women who came to Maryland in the 1600s were indentured servants. Like male indentured servants, they faced hard times in their first few years in Maryland. If a woman survived hard work and disease in the 1600s, she could be choosy about marrying, because there were three times as many English men as women in Maryland!

Maryland's colonial women worked hard to help make new homes, raise children, and create successful tobacco farms. Some women, like Margaret Brent, succeeded on their own without a husband. In the 1700s, a woman named Mary Katherine Goddard continued her husband's printing business in Baltimore after he died. She published her own newspaper, and during the American Revolution she printed the copies of the Declaration of Independence that were distributed in Maryland.

20

Besides tobacco, another important industry in Maryland was iron ore. Baltimore County was a center for the colonial iron industry. Charles Ridgeley became wealthy selling iron to England. He built one of the finest homes in colonial America on his 24,000-acre plantation near Baltimore.

Maryland clay was made into bricks that went into other fine homes in the Chesapeake Bay area. Though Annapolis never became a large city, its elegant homes were models for other Chesapeake towns.

The city of Baltimore had been founded in 1729. In the decades before the Revolution, sleepy Baltimore became one of America's biggest cities, thanks to its large harbor. Ships crowded the harbor, bringing in goods from around the world and sending out colonial products like tobacco.

Most settlers in Maryland lived in the eastern part of the colony, along Chesapeake Bay or one of the region's many rivers. Mountains covered with thick forests filled the northern and western parts of the colony. Few people lived there until around 1730, when Germans from Pennsylvania began settling there.

Interesting Fact

▶ In 1694, Maryland's capital was moved from Saint Marys to Annapolis. It wasn't until the next century that Baltimore began to be an important town, because of its tobacco industry and lots of waterfront trade.

George Washington served the British in the French and Indian War. Here he is shown reading a prayer to his troops before battle.

As Maryland grew, so did its slave population. Some free blacks who had been indentured servants lived in Maryland. But their rights and numbers decreased as slavery became common. Many of Maryland's free blacks moved to Virginia or Delaware, where they had a better chance to own land.

By the 1700s, enslaved people were being brought directly from Africa to Maryland. In the 1750s, Maryland was home to about 75,000 white people and 32,000 enslaved African-American workers.

During the 18th century, France and Great Britain competed for control of the rich farmland and fur trade in the Ohio River valley. In 1754, this competition turned into the French and Indian War. A young officer named George Washington commanded Fort Cumberland in western Maryland. By the time the fighting ended in 1763, the British had won control of Canada and some lands east of the Mississippi River.

Fighting the war had left Britain deeply in debt. For the next few years, the British tried to make the colonists pay more taxes to make up for the cost of the war. Marylanders always opposed these taxes because their colony's charter stated they would owe the king no taxes. Like other colonists, many Marylanders were feeling less like English people and more like Americans.

A Man of Many Talents

MOST AFRICAN-AMERICANS IN COLONIAL MARYLAND were enslaved workers. Some blacks, however, were either born to free parents or bought their own freedom. Benjamin Banneker was born to a freed slave in 1731. Banneker farmed tobacco and became interested in math and science.

When Banneker was a young man, he borrowed a pocket watch from a neighbor. He took the watch apart to sketch all the pieces. Then he put it back together and returned it. Using his drawings, Banneker carved exact wooden copies of the watch pieces and put them together. He made a wooden clock that ran perfectly! Over the years, Banneker continued to teach himself much about math and science.

In 1789, a national capital was being planned in the new city of Washington. President George Washington hired Banneker to help survey the land and plan the city. Banneker also published books with weather and astronomy predictions and worked to end slavery. He died in 1806.

Central Islip Public Library
33 Hawthorne Avenue
Central Islip, NY 11722

23

Chapter FOUR

Maryland Goes to War

The French and Indian war proved costly for the British. After it was over, they came upon the idea of reducing their debt by taxing the colonists.

TO PAY FOR THE COST OF THE FRENCH AND Indian War, the British passed a new tax in 1765 called the Stamp Act. Under this law, all legal documents and printed material such as newspapers had to have special stamps attached to them. The colonists would have to buy the stamps. When the new tax collector

Most of the colonists found the idea of being taxed by Britain outrageous, and many reacted violently.

reached Annapolis from England, angry crowds attacked the ship. The next ship, which was carrying the stamps, didn't stay. It headed back to England, and the law was ended.

The British tried other ways to raise money from the colonists, such as taxing tea. In 1773, a group of Massachusetts colonists snuck aboard ships in Boston Harbor and dumped a cargo of tea into the water to protest this tax. This became known as the

Interesting Fact

▶ Built in the late 1700s, the current Maryland State House in Annapolis is the oldest such building in the country still being used for the purpose of lawmaking. The building's dome still has its original "Franklin" lightning rod, too. Designed by Benjamin Franklin, the pointed rod was a powerful symbol to colonists of their independence from England.

The owner of the Peggy Stewart *named his ship after his daughter, but he was the one who ordered it set afire. Burning the ship with all its tea still onboard was the most dramatic act against British rule in all of Maryland's colonial history.*

Interesting Fact

▸ The Maryland colonists were enraged to discover that the *Peggy Stewart* was carrying more than 2,300 pounds (1,044 kg) of tea. Fearing for his family's safety, the ship's owner set the vessel—and all the tea—on fire. It burned to bits in Annapolis Harbor as the colonists watched.

Boston Tea Party. The following year, a ship called the *Peggy Stewart* was destroyed in Annapolis Harbor when it was found to be carrying a large load of tea.

That same year, the Maryland Assembly chose **delegates** to attend the first meeting of the **Continental Congress** in Philadelphia, Pennsylvania. The new Congress created an army to protect the colonists from the British. Maryland delegate Thomas Johnson recommended that his friend George Washington head the Continental army.

The first battles of the Revolution were fought in Massachusetts in 1775. Maryland sent 1,500 soldiers to Massachusetts to help in the fight. Then, on July 4, 1776, the Continental Congress issued the Declaration of Independence. But the day before, on July 3, the Maryland Assembly had issued its own declaration of independence. It said the people of Maryland "owe no **allegiance**" to the British king, who had broken the colony's charter.

Maryland had a new state **constitution** by November 1776. It featured one law that, unfortunately, wouldn't last for long: Free African-American men had the right to vote.

Maryland soldiers fought bravely in the Revolutionary War. Many died at a battle in Long Island, New York, in 1776. At sea, Maryland ships captured many British ships. The courage shown by the Maryland soldiers made them favorites of General Washington. Maryland got its state nickname—the Old Line State—because Maryland's "line" of soldiers was so reliable.

In December 1776, the Continental Congress moved from Philadelphia to Baltimore, where they felt

After fighting alongside the British in 1754, General Washington led the colonists against them in the Revolutionary War 21 years later. Here he reviews the troops of the Continental army shortly after taking charge.

▶ It is believed that Maryland's "Old Line" nickname came directly from a battle in which 400 troops in the First Maryland Regiment held off 10,000 British soldiers. This helped George Washington and his men escape.

it was safer. They stayed until March 1777. Few battles took place in Maryland during the war, but homes and sometimes entire villages were destroyed by British soldiers who sailed up rivers from Chesapeake Bay.

Finally, in January 1783, Great Britain and the United States signed a peace treaty. The Continental Congress approved the treaty in Annapolis in the new statehouse, which had been completed in 1774. Congress met in the Annapolis statehouse for nine months until it moved to New York. In the coming years, the 13 new states would form a government for the new country.

The Continental army faced many hardships and had to retreat often. But because of the gritty determination of soldiers such as the Marylanders, the American colonies eventually won their freedom.

AMERICANS WHO SUPPORTED THE REVOLUTIONARY War took a big chance. They might lose their land or even their lives if caught by the British. Maryland's Charles Carroll (left as a younger man; below when he was older) was wealthy, and he had much to lose. But he wasn't afraid to take a stand for liberty.

Carroll was a delegate to the Continental Congress. When he signed his name to the Declaration of Independence, another man commented, "There go several millions." He meant that Carroll could lose his fortune. Someone else told Carroll not

to worry, because Charles Carroll was a common name. The British wouldn't know which one to arrest. So, below his name, Carroll boldly added "of Carrollton," to say where he lived. "They cannot mistake me now," he declared. Carroll survived the Revolutionary War. He lived until 1832, longer than any other signer of the Declaration of Independence.

Chapter FIVE

First Steps of a Nation

TALKING ABOUT AND FIGHTING FOR FREEDOM from Great Britain made many Americans think harder about slavery. Shouldn't freedom be for everyone? Though southern states weren't about to change, many northern states had taken steps to outlaw slavery. Maryland, the northernmost "southern"

As Maryland's governing body changed and grew over the years, so did the State House where the lawmakers worked. The third State House, shown here and still standing today, was the first of the three to house the representatives of a free nation.

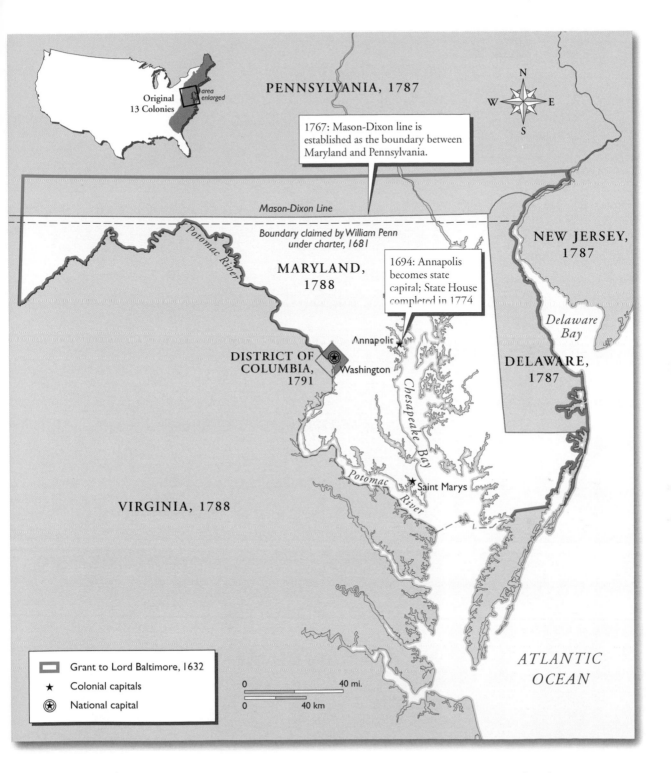

PENNSYLVANIA, 1787

1767: Mason-Dixon line is established as the boundary between Maryland and Pennsylvania.

Mason-Dixon Line

Boundary claimed by William Penn under charter, 1681

Potomac River

MARYLAND, 1788

1694: Annapolis becomes state capital; State House completed in 1774

NEW JERSEY, 1787

Delaware Bay

DISTRICT OF COLUMBIA, 1791

Annapolis

Washington

DELAWARE, 1787

Chesapeake Bay

VIRGINIA, 1788

Potomac River

Saint Marys

ATLANTIC OCEAN

Original 13 Colonies

area enlarged

N
W   E
S

Grant to Lord Baltimore, 1632

★ Colonial capitals

⊛ National capital

0   40 mi.
0   40 km

Maryland Colony before statehood

state, still allowed slavery. But in 1783, it outlawed importing more enslaved people.

Before the Revolutionary War was even over, the states had worked out a form of government for their new nation. Called the Articles of Confederation, it provided for a very weak central government. The national government did not even have the power to tax, so it had no way of raising money.

Though Maryland was now a state, there were still some questions about its boundaries. This time, the disagreement involved the neighboring state of Virginia. Which state had rights to which parts of the Potomac River? In 1785, a meeting between representatives of the two states solved the issue.

General Washington resigned at a meeting in Annapolis, Maryland. The problems of the young nation would eventually call him to service again.

This success led to Maryland inviting all of the former colonies to another meeting. Delegates from New York, New Jersey, Virginia, Delaware, and Pennsylvania came to Annapolis in 1786. They decided to hold a national meeting to discuss weaknesses of the Articles of Confederation.

This meeting was held in Philadelphia in 1787. After four months of arguing, a new government was born, spelled out in the newly written Constitution.

The people at the meeting became divided between federalists, who favored a strong national government, and anti-federalists, who wanted the states to have more power. A Maryland delegate, Luther Martin, became a leader of the anti-federalists. Anti-federalists feared that bigger states such as Virginia or New York might end up controlling the national government. They thought smaller states would have little power.

Luther Martin was a prominent Maryland lawyer. During the Constitutional Convention he fought for the rights of the smaller states.

▸ Nearly 100 years after the 1785 boundary agreement, Maryland and Virginia were still squabbling over which state owned which parts of the Potomac River. After the Civil War (1861–1865), each state even set up its own "navy" to guard its fishing industry from the other.

In the end, the federalists won. The Constitution gave broad powers to the national government. Luther Martin left Philadelphia without signing the Constitution.

The Constitution had to be approved by at least nine states to become law. Despite Martin's objections, Maryland approved the Constitution in April 1788. It was the seventh state to do so.

Some people who thought the Constitution gave too much power to the central government insisted that a list of the rights of individuals be added to the Constitution. The **Bill of Rights** was approved in 1791 to serve that purpose.

The Philadelphia meeting of 1787, known as the Constitutional Convention, was suggested by Maryland representatives to address the problems not solved by the Articles of Confederation. Once again George Washington found himself serving the young nation when he was chosen to preside over the Convention.

In 1783, Maryland had suggested that Annapolis become home to the new national government. Though it was turned down, the state later made another generous offer. Maryland and Virginia each donated land along the Potomac River that became the District of Columbia, the new national capital. Maryland also gave money to help construct government buildings.

Maryland's early contributions to the United States of America were many. It was the first colony to value religious freedom. It provided brave soldiers during the Revolutionary War. And it helped provide the land on which the nation's government does business to this day.

Maryland and Virginia both donated land for the nation's capital, which was named Washington, D.C. It was called "District of Columbia" for Christopher Columbus. The portion of D.C. donated by Virginia was later given back to that state.

1500s   Piscataway, Nanticoke, Pocomoke, Wicomico, Patuxent, and Susquehannock live in what is now Maryland.

1632   King Charles I of England grants a charter for a new colony called Maryland to George Calvert.

1634   The ships the *Ark* and the *Dove* bring the first English settlers to Maryland; Saint Marys is established as Maryland's first capital.

1635   Maryland's General Assembly meets for the first time.

1649   The General Assembly passes the Act of Religious Toleration.

1694   Annapolis becomes the capital of Maryland.

1763   Great Britain defeats France in the French and Indian War.

1765   The British pass the Stamp Act; many colonists protest it, and it is ended.

1767   The Mason-Dixon Line is established as the boundary between Maryland and Pennsylvania.

1774   Maryland colonists destroy a cargo of tea aboard the *Peggy Stewart* to protest a tax on tea; the First Continental Congress meets in Philadelphia, Pennsylvania.

1776   The Declaration of Independence is signed; in December, the Continental Congress moves to Baltimore as the British army closes in on Philadelphia.

1783   The United States and Great Britain sign a peace treaty, ending the Revolutionary War.

1788   Maryland becomes the seventh state to approve the U.S. Constitution.

1791   Maryland and Virginia contribute land to form the District of Columbia.

allegiance (uh-LEE-junss)
Allegiance is loyalty to a government. Maryland passed a declaration of independence, which said that the people of Maryland owed no allegiance to Great Britain because the king had broken the colony's charter.

assembly (uh-SEM-blee)
An assembly is a part of government that makes laws. Maryland's General Assembly formed in 1635.

Bill of Rights (BILL of RITES)
The Bill of Rights is a list of individual rights that are protected, such as freedom of speech and freedom of religion. The Bill of Rights is the first 10 amendments, or changes, to the U.S. Constitution.

charter (CHAR-tur)
A charter is a document giving settlers permission to form a colony. George Calvert received a charter for Maryland in 1632.

constitution (kon-stuh-TOO-shuhn)
A constitution is a document outlining the basic laws and structure of a government. Maryland approved the U.S. Constitution in 1788.

Continental Congress (kon-tuh-NEN-tuhl KONG-riss)
The Continental Congress was a meeting of colonists that served as the American government during Revolutionary times. The Continental Congress moved from Philadelphia to Baltimore for four months during the Revolution.

delegates (DEL-uh-guhts)
Delegates are people who represent other people at a meeting. Thomas Johnson was a delegate from Maryland at the First Continental Congress.

indentured servants (in-DEN-churd SER-vuhnts)
Indentured servants were people who agreed to work for someone else for a certain period of time in exchange for payment of travel expenses. Many of Maryland's first settlers were indentured servants.

noblemen (NOH-buhl-men)
Noblemen were leading members of society. The founders of Maryland were Roman Catholic noblemen.

plantations (plan-TAY-shuhns)
Plantations were large farms that grew a single important crop and usually used enslaved workers. Most plantations in Maryland grew tobacco.

Maryland Colony's FOUNDING FATHERS

Charles Carroll (known as Charles Carroll of Carrollton) (1737–1832)
Continental Congress delegate, Aug., 1776–78; Declaration of Independence signer; U.S. senator, 1789–92

Daniel Carroll (1730–1796)
Continental Congress delegate, 1781–83; Articles of Confederation signer, 1781; Constitutional Convention delegate, 1787; U.S. Constitution signer

Samuel Chase (1741–1811)
Continental Congress delegate, 1774–1778, 1784, 1785; Declaration of Independence signer; U.S. Supreme Court associate justice, 1796–1811; impeached 1804, acquitted 1805

John Hanson (1715–1783)
Continental Congress delegate, 1780–82; Articles of Confederation signer; first president of congress under the Articles of Confederation, 1781–82

Luther Martin (1748?–1826)
Continental Congress delegate, 1785; Constitutional Convention delegate, 1787; fought ratification of the Constitution through 1788; Maryland state attorney general, 1778–1805, 1818–22

James McHenry (1753–1816)
Private secretary to General George Washington, 1778–80; Continental Congress delegate, 1783–86; Constitutional Convention delegate, 1787; U.S. secretary of war, 1796–1800; Fort McHenry in Baltimore named for him

John F. Mercer (1759–1821)
Continental Congress delegate, 1782; U.S. House of Representatives member, 1791–94; Maryland governor, 1801–03

William Paca (1740–1799)
Continental Congress delegate, 1774–79; Declaration of Independence signer; Maryland chief justice, 1778; Maryland governor, 1782–85; U.S. district court justice for Maryland, 1789–99

Thomas Stone (1743–1787)
Continental Congress delegate, 1775–78, 1783; Declaration of Independence signer

Dan of St. Thomas Jenifer (1723–1790)
Continental Congress delegate, 1778–82; Constitutional Convention delegate, 1787; U.S. Constitution signer

For Further INFORMATION

Web Sites

Visit our homepage for lots of links about the Maryland colony:
http://www.childsworld.com/links.html

Note to Parents, Teachers, and Librarians:
We routinely verify our Web links to make sure they're safe,
active sites—so encourage your readers to check them out!

Books

Burgan, Michael. *Maryland.* Danbury, Conn.: Children's Press, 1999.

Jensen, Ann. *Leonard Calvert and the Maryland Adventure.* Centreville, Md.:
Tidewater Publishers, 1998.

Rauth, Leslie. *Maryland.* New York: Benchmark Books, 2000.

Places to Visit or Contact

The Banneker-Douglass Museum
To learn more about African-American life in Maryland
84 Franklin Street
Annapolis, MD 21401
410/974-2893

Maryland Office of Tourism Development
For information on sites to visit all over Maryland
217 East Redwood Street, 9th Floor
Baltimore, MD 21202
410/767-3400

State Library Resource Center
For all kinds of books, documents, and videos about Maryland
Enoch Pratt Free Library
400 Cathedral Street
Baltimore, MD 21201
410/396-5430

Index

About the Author

JEAN KINNEY WILLIAMS LIVES AND WRITES IN CINCINNATI, Ohio. Her nonfiction books for children include *Matthew Henson: Polar Adventurer* and a series of books about American religions, which include *The Amish, The Shakers, The Mormons, The Quakers,* and *The Christian Scientists.* She is also the author of *The Pony Express* and *African-Americans in the Colonies.*

AUG 20 2004 ✓R.S.

CENTRAL ISLIP PUBLIC LIBRARY

3 1800 00210 4905